W9-BMP-892

LINCOLN SCHOOL

437221

Taylor, Barbara
Cobras

597.96 TAY

PREDATORS
COBRAS

Barbara Taylor

LINCOLN SCHOOL
LIBRARY MEDIA CENTER
MUNDELEIN, IL

RAINTREE
STECK-VAUGHN
PUBLISHERS

A Harcourt Company

Austin   New York
www.raintreesteckvaughn.com

© Copyright 2003, text, Steck-Vaughn Company

All rights reserved. No part of this book may be reproduced or utilized in any form or by any means, electronic or mechanical, including photocopying, recording, or by any information storage and retrieval system, without permission in writing from the Publishers. Inquiries should be addressed to:

Copyright Permissions
Steck-Vaughn Company
P.O. Box 26015
Austin, TX 78755

Published by Raintree Steck-Vaughn Publishers, an imprint of Steck-Vaughn Company

Library of Congress Cataloging-in-Publication Data

Cataloging-in-publication data is available at the Library of Congress.

ISBN 0-7398-6599-4

Acknowledgements
The publishers would like to thank the following for permission to reproduce photographs:
CORBIS Corporation/Images: pages 13 top, 18; 25 right (Karen Su); 27 (Christine Kolisch); 29 (Bojan Brecelj). Gallo Images/Anthony Bannister Photo Library: pages 5, 12, 23 bottom; pages 2, 10 (Daryl Balfour); 3, 17 bottom (Nigel J. Dennis); 5, 7 top, 8, 8–9, 30, 31 (Rod Patterson); 9 (Tim Jackson); 11 top, 17 top (Peter Lillie); 20 (Lex Hes); 23 top (Dirk Heinrich); 25 left (Keith Begg); Robert C. Nunnington. Frank Lane Photo Agency: pages 11 bottom (Jurgen & Christine Sohns); 19 bottom (M. Ranjit); 26 (Michael Gore). Natural History Photo Agency: pages 4 (Hellio & Van Ingen); 1, 4–5, 16, 19 top, 21 top and bottom, 22, 24 (Daniel Heuclin); 13 (Pavel German); 15 (Andy Rouse). Ecoscene/Papilio: pages 7 bottom (Robert Pickett); 14 (Clive Druet). Cover photos: Ecoscene (DETAILS TO INSERT)

Printed in China/Hong Kong

07 06 05 04 03
10 9 8 7 6 5 4 3 2 1

LOOK FOR THE PREDATOR

Look for the cobra in boxes like this. Here you will find extra facts, stories, and other interesting information about cobras.

CONTENTS

WHAT ARE COBRAS?

Cobras are very poisonous snakes famous for their deadly bite. They use their poison, which is called venom, to stun their prey or to defend themselves against predators.

Cobras are members of the *Elapid* family of snakes, which all have short fangs fixed at the front of the mouth in the top jaw. There are more than 270 different kinds of cobras and their relatives in the *Elapid* family.

◀ Cobras are recognized by the hood on their neck, which they spread out when they are angry or disturbed. This is an Indian cobra.

Snakes belong to a group of animals called reptiles. Reptiles are covered in tough, waterproof scales that overlap like tiles on a roof. A snake's scales are extra-thick pieces of skin made of keratin—the same material as your fingernails. Several times a year, snakes shed their old skin to reveal a bright, shiny, new skin underneath.

All snakes are predators, or hunters, that eat prey such as lizards, rats, birds, fish—and other snakes! As reptiles they lay eggs, although some sea snakes give birth to live young. Snakes can live for up to 30 years.

▶ Cobras can lift up the front part of their body to look for danger or to appear more threatening.

COBRA FAMILY

The *Elapid* family includes the mambas, the coral snakes, the kraits, and the many Australian snakes, including the taipan and the tiger snakes. Many sea snakes are also in the *Elapid* snake family.

◀ This sea krait glides through the water in S-shaped curves searching for fish to eat. Its flattened tail works like the oar on a rowboat to push it along.

KILLING MACHINE

A cobra's body is a long, thin tube that is dry, not slimy, to the touch. It has no legs, so it wriggles, slithers, and slides along. It does not have horns, spikes, or body armor for protection, although its scales do help to protect its soft body.

What a cobra does have is poisonous venom. This helps it to kill its prey quickly, without having to fight a long battle in which it might be injured. All the important parts of a cobra are in the head. The tongue flicks in and out to taste and smell the air. The eyes watch all around, and the ears inside the head pick up quiet sounds.

RECORD BREAKER

Imagine a snake that is longer than most crocodiles. The king cobra is this long. It is the world's longest poisonous snake, reaching lengths of up to 18 feet (5.58 meters). Its head is as big as an adult's hand and it can stretch up high enough to look you straight in the eye.

▼ The king cobra has a long, narrow hood, without patterns of any kind, unlike true cobras. Its smooth scales help it to slide along quickly as it chases its prey.

LINCOLN SCHOOL
LIBRARY MEDIA CENTER
MUNDELEIN, IL

▲Cobras have a slender body, a long tail, large eyes, and a tendency to lift their head off the ground to search for prey. These are all characteristics of active hunters.

◀ A cobra's hood is made from flaps of skin supported by long ribs. The white circle on a monocled cobra's hood looks like a big eye. This helps to distract predators or frighten them away.

The rest of the body contains long, thin organs such as the heart, lungs, kidneys, and liver. The stomach and gut are very stretchy so they can hold large meals. This means the cobra can eat as much as possible at each meal, which is important because there may be gaps of several months between meals.

WHERE COBRAS LIVE

Cobras and their relatives are usually found in hot, tropical places because they rely on heat from their surroundings to warm them up. In cool weather, cobras slow down and become inactive, only moving when the temperature rises.

Cobras are found in Africa, southern Asia, and Australia. Their relatives, the coral snakes, live in the United States. Snakes in the cobra family live in forests, grasslands, deserts, swamps, and the sea. They also live near people. The place where an animal lives is called its habitat.

▼The Egyptian cobra is especially common near oases and villages. It mainly eats lizards and sometimes lives in lizards' holes.

▶The cape cobra from southern Africa lives in dry habitats like this.

ALARMING AUSTRALIA

In most parts of the world, the number of snakes belonging to the cobra family is fairly small. But in Australia, cobras and their relatives make up 60 percent of snakes. This is the only place in the world where poisonous snakes outnumber the harmless ones.

Most land-based cobras live on the ground, but in Africa there are cobras and mambas that live in trees. The king cobras of Asia are good at climbing trees as well as being excellent swimmers. They often live near rain forest streams, where the temperature and humidity stay pretty much the same year round.

▼ Only a few cobras live underground, but many find shelter in holes and crevices. This cape cobra is sticking its head out of the sand in the Kalahari Desert.

COBRA FOOD

Cobras eat a lot of other snakes and large lizards but also feed on frogs, birds, and small mammals such as rats and mice. They are often found near where people live because there are plenty of rats to eat. Sea snakes and water cobras prefer fish as prey.

WHEN IS A WORM NOT A WORM?

The Australian death adder has a brightly colored tip on its tail that looks like a worm. It wriggles this "worm" to lure lizards, birds, and small mammals within reach of its deadly poisonous fangs.

▼ Cobras usually hunt on the ground, but some climb trees in search of prey.

King cobras eat mainly other snakes. They usually prey on nonvenomous snakes, for example, Asian rat snakes and pythons. They will also eat very poisonous snakes such as Indian cobras, kraits, and even smaller king cobras. King cobras seem to be immune to the venom of their poisonous prey. Strange as it may seem, the king cobra will often share its sleeping quarters with potential prey!

▲ This cape cobra is searching a bird's nest for baby birds to eat.

Baby cobras are ready to hunt after they first shed their skin at about a week old. They have fully formed fangs and venom glands, and their venom is just as strong as an adult's. However, baby cobras cannot eat as big prey as their parents. In proportion to their size, snakes eat bigger meals than any other predator on land.

▼ Rat snakes are typical prey for snakes in the cobra family.

FANGS AND POISONS

A cobra's main weapons are its two venomous fangs; these are extra large teeth with sharp points on the end. These teeth are fixed to the top jaw and cannot move. A cobra's fangs are almost an inch long.

If the fangs were any longer, the snake would bite through its lower jaw. Snakes in the viper family have longer fangs, but these can be folded back against the roof of the mouth. A snake's fangs are hollow and linked to bags of venom in the head, behind the eyes. The venom bags are special glands that in many other animals produce saliva, a juice that helps digest food. The venom itself is a clear, pale yellow fluid. As the venom is used up, the snake makes more, so it never runs out. Cobras are immune to their own venom.

DEADLY VENOM

The venom in one bite from an Australian taipan snake is enough to kill up to 12,000 guinea pigs. The fierce snake, or inland taipan, has perhaps the most toxic venom of any snake. The venom in just one bite of this snake would be enough to kill more than 100 people or 250,000 mice!

▶ A South African rinkhal, a spitting cobra, in an attacking pose, about to strike its prey.

▲ This skull of a king cobra shows the large fangs in the upper jaw. The jaws open very wide to swallow prey whole.

Behind the fangs and in the lower jaw, cobras have short, sharp teeth that curve backwards. These are good for gripping and holding prey; a cobra does not have any chewing teeth. None of the teeth are strong and they often get broken, so they are continually being replaced. New fangs move into place before the old ones are lost. This means that a snake may have two fangs on each side of its jaw for a short time.

▲ Antivenin injected into a person's bloodstream helps defeat a cobra's poisonous venom.

COBRA SENSES

The most important senses for cobras and most other snakes are smell and taste. They do not rely as much on sight and hearing as we do. Snakes are one of the few animals to taste and smell with their tongues.

In the roof of a snake's mouth is an organ called the Jacobson's organ that analyzes tastes and smells collected by the tongue. It opens into the mouth by two small holes like nostrils. The snake presses one fork of its tongue into each opening, which is why snakes have a forked tongue.

A snake's eyes are always wide open because they do not have any eyelids. Snakes cannot blink or close their eyes. Each eye is protected by a transparent scale called a spectacle. It is difficult to know if snakes can see colors, but there is evidence that at least some of them can.

▼ King cobras appear to be more intelligent than other cobras. Zookeepers say they learn faster than other snakes and can tell their keepers apart from strangers.

▶ A snake's forked tongue collects chemicals from the air to find out about food, mates, predators, and any other interesting things happening nearby. Through a small notch in its upper jaw, a snake can put out its tongue without opening its mouth.

GOOD VIBRATIONS

Many people think that snakes are deaf, but they do have one ear bone joined to the jaw. They can pick up sound vibrations through the ground and probably some low sounds traveling through the air.

GOING HUNTING

Cobras are active hunters that chase their prey rather than waiting to ambush it. They hunt mainly by smell, "tasting" the air with their forked tongues.

Cobras track their prey carefully to get as close as possible. They slither and slide along the ground or the branch of a tree, or wriggle through the water, until they are a few inches away. Then they quickly attack. They strike with their fangs and overcome their prey with a huge dose of venom.

NEW GLASSES

King cobras see clearly up to 300 feet (100 meters) away but they do not rely on sight when hunting. This is just as well because when they shed their skin, they suffer from poor eyesight for up to 10 days while new eye coverings (like contact lenses) form.

► Cobras try to get as near to their prey as they can, relying on eyesight only for the final approach.

▲ This African Cape cobra is gliding toward the nest of sociable weaver birds.

Most cobras hunt in the evening but they will also hunt during the day. The king cobra's round pupils let in lots of light, which is useful when it hunts in daylight. Nocturnal snakes, which only hunt at night, usually have vertical pupils because these can be closed more tightly than a circular pupil during the day. This protects the snake's sensitive eyes from bright light during the day.

▼ Cobras can chase their prey for a long distance, moving forward rapidly with the head raised off the ground.

IN FOR THE KILL

When a cobra comes in for the kill, it raises its body and strikes straight down, usually making a sharp hissing sound. Its fangs pierce the victim's skin and it pumps venom down the hollow fangs and into the victim's body.

Cobras tend to hang onto their prey with their teeth until they are sure enough poison has entered the wound. The longer the snake bites or the deeper it bites, the more venom is injected.

ROYAL DEATH

A king cobra's venom is less toxic than a common cobra's. But a king cobra delivers more venom with each bite—enough to kill an elephant or 20 people. The king cobra causes only about five human deaths a year—rattlesnakes in North America kill about 25 people a year.

▼An Egyptian banded cobra slides through the grass toward its prey.

LINCOLN SCHOOL
LIBRARY MEDIA CENTER
MUNDELEIN, IL

Cobra venom contains a mixture of poisons.
Most of the poisons cause breathing or heart problems,
or paralysis. This keeps the prey still while the snake swallows
its meal. Other poisons start digesting the paralyzed victim.

Cobras have no limbs to tear food and their teeth cannot chop
and chew food into smaller pieces. They gulp down every meal
whole. Special loose jaws allow the snake to open its mouth
really wide. Then the jaws "walk" from side to side over the
food to force it down the snake's throat.

▲ This cobra is a cannibal because it is eating another cobra of its own kind. It may take several days or even weeks to digest its meal.

▶ Snakes are easy for king cobras to swallow because they slide down the throat smoothly. A snake can usually swallow its prey in 10 to 20 minutes, although a large meal may take an hour to swallow.

COLOR AND CAMOUFLAGE

The colors of cobras and other snakes come from pigments inside the scales and the way light reflects off the scales. When a snake's skin is stretched, such as by a cobra spreading its hood, the scales pull apart so you can see the skin between the scales. The skin may be a different color from the scales.

Typical cobras have spotted brown, black, and sandy colors that make them difficult to see, especially when they hide under bushes or in the undergrowth. In forests king cobras have darker skins, and in open forests or on plains they have lighter skins. These camouflage colors help them to hide from prey or enemies.

FALSE COLORS

Milk snakes and false coral snakes are not poisonous but they copy the warning colors of coral snakes. Predators leave them alone, too, rather than risk being bitten.

◀ The colors and patterns of the Egyptian cobra are hard to spot among the dry grass and rocks where it lives.

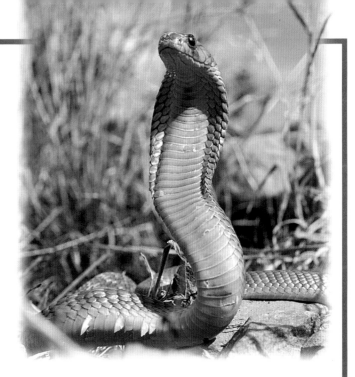

▶ A gold cobra is hard to see against the dry desert grass.

Some members of the cobra family, such as kraits and coral snakes, are striped with much brighter colors. These stripes warn predators to leave the snakes alone because they are poisonous. They are called warning colors.

▶ Most kraits have bold black-and-white or black-and-yellow stripes to warn that their venom is very toxic. Kraits come out at night and feed mainly on other snakes.

SELF-DEFENSE

Cobras have many enemies, such as mongooses and people. Wild boar and mongooses steal cobra eggs, and baby cobras may be eaten by army ants, giant centipedes, and civet cats.

Cobras usually try to escape enemies by keeping still or crawling under rocks or into a hole. But if they have to fight, cobras rear up and spread the hood wide to scare enemies away. The huge hood also makes a cobra look too big for an enemy to swallow. Cobras only bite as a last resort, if they fail to scare a predator. Mambas have no hood, but they can inflate their throat instead.

Cobras may also hiss loudly to make themselves even more frightening. The hiss is produced by air passing through tiny holes in the snake's windpipe. A King cobra's hiss sounds a lot like a dog growling.

▼ Mongooses usually win fights with cobras because of their speed, agility, and timing. Cobras are slower than many snakes and the mongoose's thick coat helps to protect it against the snake's fangs.

◀ This is a western black spitting cobra defending its eggs. Unless they are defending their eggs or young, cobras are more likely to slither away than to attack.

Several African cobras do more than hiss and show a scary hood. They spray venom through small slits at the tips of their fangs. They only spit venom to defend themselves and give themselves time to escape, not to catch prey. One spitting cobra, the rinkhals, will even "play dead" at first, since predators prefer live prey and may leave it alone. If this does not work, it will come back to life and spit venom instead.

SUPER SPIT

A spitting cobra can spray its venom more than six feet (2 meters). It aims directly into an attacker's eyes and its aim is deadly accurate.

▶ Here venom streams from a spitting cobra's fangs. If venom gets in the eyes, it causes a burning pain and blindness that may last for several hours or even be permanent.

23

UNDER THREAT

The biggest threat to cobras and other snakes comes from people, who often kill the reptiles through fear and ignorance.

People build houses and farms on land where snakes live. Snakes are often killed by vehicles on roads. They are also killed for meat or for entertainment. Farmers, not knowing that cobras and other snakes can help them by eating pests, kill snakes to protect their farm animals and workers.

▼ An Indian cobra being captured by people who are trying to protect their village and animals.

In some countries, snakes are killed so parts of their bodies, such as their skin, meat, and bile, can be used in medicines. Cobras are killed for their beautiful skins, which are made into belts, purses, shoes, and other luxury items. In one year, more than ten million snakes were killed in India for the skin industry.

To help cobras and other snakes survive, people need to learn more about them and take action to save their habitats. Snakes and people do not mix well together so the snakes need undisturbed habitats well away from people where they can live and hunt in their natural environment.

COBRA KILLERS

In India about 10,000 people a year die from snakebites, mostly from the bites of the spectacled cobra. About 10 percent of cobra bites kill people when antivenin is not available.

▲ This is a python skin. Snake skins are traded illegally and tourists caught bringing them back from vacations can be heavily fined.

◄ Cobras are beautiful, shy, secretive snakes that are not as dangerous as people think. They will not usually attack people unless they feel threatened.

25

COBRA FACTS

Here is a selection of interesting facts and figures about cobras.

FIRST SNAKES

The first snakes appeared between 100 and 150 million years ago alongside the dinosaurs. The cobra family did not evolve until the Miocene Period, which lasted from 24.6 million to 5.1 million years ago. Nowadays there are some 2,700 different kinds of snakes but less than a quarter of them are poisonous. Only 300 of these poisonous snakes, including members of the cobra family, are able to kill people.

WORSHIPING COBRAS

The cobra symbol has been found on seals in the ruins of Mohenjo-Daro, in southern Pakistan, an ancient city about 4,000 years old. In India the cobra has been widely worshiped since ancient times. Hindu mythology depicts a cobra-race called Nagas, who inhabit the underworld, *Nagalok* or *Patala*. Manasa or Durgamma, queen of the Nagas, is worshiped by women to protect their children from snakebite. On the Hindu festival of *Nagapanchami,* people pour milk and even blood on images of cobras and down snake holes. King cobras have also been worshiped as sun gods, with power over rain, thunder, and fertility.

◄ Snake charmers do not really hypnotize cobras with their flute music. Instead the cobra follows the movements of the pipe, swaying from side to side. Often the snakes are exhausted or have had their fangs removed.

CREATION COBRAS

A Hindu creation myth describes a gigantic cobra named Shesha who sheltered the god Vishnu. Shesha had from five to 1,000 heads. When he yawned, massive earthquakes happened and fire and venom from his mouth caused destruction on Earth.

COBRAS IN THE MOVIES

The cobra is also a very popular theme in Indian films. Usually, the cobra is shown as a guardian of goodness and a destroyer of the wicked. Many films are based on the myth of the Icchadari cobras, which are said to have the power to take on a human form and to have one devoted mate. If the mate is killed, the cobra is able to see the image of the killer in the dead snake's eyes and sets off on a trail of revenge.

COMFORTING COBRAS

The African Leitayo tribe will never kill a cobra because they believe that a cobra will comfort a woman about to give birth. The cobra is supposed to stay with the woman until a day after the child is born to see that all is well. It is then given milk to drink, after which it leaves. The Leitayo maintain that cobras are members of their tribe and so will not harm tribefolk.

CLEOPATRA'S COBRA

The Egyptian cobra is famous for being the asp that Queen Cleopatra of ancient Egypt used to commit suicide. It is likely that Cleopatra chose this snake because it has a quick-acting venom. A real asp is just as poisonous, but causes a slow and painful death.

▼ A Buddhist story describes how a massive cobra spread its hood over the Buddha to protect him from the sun while he meditated. Cobra images guard the entrances of many Buddhist and Hindu temples.

COBRA WORDS

This glossary explains some of the words used in this book that you might not have seen before.

Antivenin
A medicine used to treat a snakebite. It is made by injecting a horse (or other mammal) with treated snake venom so the horse's blood produces antibodies against the venom.

Cannibal
An animal that eats others of its species or type.

Camouflage
Colors or patterns that allow a snake to blend in with its surroundings.

Cold-blooded
An animal whose temperature varies with that of its surroundings.

Cobras
Poisonous snakes in the *Elapid* family, with short, fixed fangs at the front of the mouth.

Dormant period
A resting period when an animal's or a plant's body shuts down to help it survive harsh times.

◀ **This Egyptian cobra has an extended hood.**

Elapids
A group of poisonous snakes that includes cobras, mambas, coral snakes, sea snakes, kraits, and many Australian snakes.

Evolve
To develop into a variety of different species over long periods of time, in response to changes in the environment.

Fang
A long, pointed tooth, which may be used to deliver venom.

Habitat
The place where an animal or a plant lives.

Hood
The skin behind a cobra's head that opens out to frighten enemies.

Jacobson's organ
Nerve pits in the roof of a snake's mouth. The pits can identify chemicals on the tongue.

Keratin
A hard substance that a snake's scales are made of.

Moult
To cast off a layer of dead skin.

Pigment
Coloring matter.

Predator
An animal that hunts other animals and eats them.

Prey
An animal that is hunted and killed by another animal—a predator— for food.

Pupil
The area in the middle of the front of the eye through which light enters.

Reptile
A cold-blooded animal with a bony skeleton and a scaly skin. Reptiles lay eggs or give birth to live young. They usually live on land.

Salivary gland
A gland in the mouth that produces a colorless liquid

The Egyptian cobra's raised head and inflated hood was often depicted on the headdresses of ancient Egyptian pharaohs. This was the symbol of the goddess Ejo. The Egyptians associated snakes with rain, fertility, and wealth.

called saliva. This helps food to slide down the throat and contains digestive juices.

Scale
Small, overlapping plates that grow out of the top layer of a reptile's skin and help to protect it.

Spectacle
A see-through scale that covers a snake's eye.

Venom
Poisonous fluid produced by some snakes to kill their prey and defend themselves from

enemies. Venom is injected into prey by biting.

Vipers
A group of poisonous snakes with fangs that fold back against the roof of the mouth.

Warning colors
Bright colors—mostly as stripes —that warn of an animal's poisonous nature.

Windpipe
The pipe that leads from the throat to the lungs, through which air enters and leaves the lungs.

COBRA PROJECTS

If you want to find out more about cobras, here are some ideas for projects.

WATCHING COBRAS

The best places to watch cobras and other snakes close up are zoos and wildlife centers. There may be demonstrations where experienced animal handlers allow you to touch and hold snakes that are not dangerous. You could take photographs or draw sketches and make notes about things such as where the snakes come from and what they eat. Look for articles in newspapers or magazines and build up a snake file with all the information you have collected.

ASK ABOUT ANTIVENIN

Some people keep pet snakes —occasionally the poisonous ones! Go to your local veterinarian's office and ask if you can speak to a vet about snake antivenin. Ask if the vet has any experience handling antivenin and if he or she has any in the office. Has the vet ever handled a cobra and was he or she nervous and why? Write a report on what you learned.

▲ This cape cobra spreads its hood in a threatening display. The hood makes it look bigger and more dangerous.

◀ This is a South African cobra, a member of the most venomous snake family.

COBRAS ON THE WEB

If you have access to the Internet, you will be able to find lots of information about snakes and cobras. Try these websites.

www.cobras.org
A good general site with lots of information about cobras and links to other sites.

**www.nationalgeographic.com/features/
97/kingcobra/index-n.html**
Information about the King cobra and its lifestyle with amazing pictures.

**www.creatures2.animallovers.co.uk/
kingcobra.html**
Information about the distribution, size, lifestyle, food, breeding, and conservation of this very special snake.

**www.worldalmanacforkids.com/explore/
animals/snake.html**
General information about all snakes, such as habitats, movement, physical characteristics, behavior, and reproduction.

HOW YOU CAN HELP

Join a conservation group to find out more about snakes and other reptiles and see how you can help snakes survive in the future. Many zoos and conservation groups have plans that allow you to sponsor rare snakes and help to pay for their upkeep.

INDEX